DIRECTORY TO COLLEGE BUILDINGS

1-7, 9-11, 14 RESIDENCES OF A PORTION OF
    THE FACULTY
8 EAST LANSING POST OFFICE
12 HOWARD TERRACE – RESIDENCE
13 WOMAN'S BUILDING – DORMITORY AND
    CLASS ROOMS
15 ASTRONOMICAL OBSERVATORY
16 COLLEGE HOSPITAL
17 U.S. WEATHER BUREAU
18 WAITING ROOM AND BOOK STORE
19 HORTICULTURAL LABORATORY
20 BACTERIOLOGICAL LABORATORY
21 LIBRARY AND MUSEUM – OFFICES OF THE
    PRESIDENT AND SECRETARY
22 BOTANICAL LABORATORY

23 FORESTRY BUILDING
24 ENTOMOLOGICAL LABORATORY
25 AGRICULTURAL BUILDING
26 WILLIAMS HALL – MEN'S DORMITORY
27 COLLEGE HALL
28 CHEMICAL LABORATORY
29 ABBOT HALL – MEN'S DORMITORY
30 BATHHOUSE
31 ARMORY
32 GREENHOUSE
33 UNION LITERARY SOCIETY BUILDING
34 WELLS HALL – MEN'S DORMITORY
35 ENGINEERING BUILDING
36 ENGINEERING SHOPS
36A FARM MECHANICS

37 VETERINARY LA[B]
38 HEATING & LIGH[T]
39 ASSAY LABORATORY
40 REPAIR SHOP & STORAGE
40A COAL STORAGE
40B STORAGE
41 HOG HOUSE
41A DETENTION BARN
42 SHEEP BARN
43 HORSE BARN
44 COMPOST SHED
45 BULL DARN
46 BEEF CATTLE BARN & SILOS
47 DAIRY BARN AND SILOS
48 IMPLEMENT BARN

56 RESIDENCE
57 HORTICULTURAL BARN
58 FRUIT HOUSE
59 DAIRY BUILDING
60 POULTRY PLANT
61 EXPERIMENT STATION BARN
62 BACTERIOLOGICAL STABLES
63 SOILS BUILDING
64 VETERINARY SURGERY & CLINIC
65 GYMNASIUM

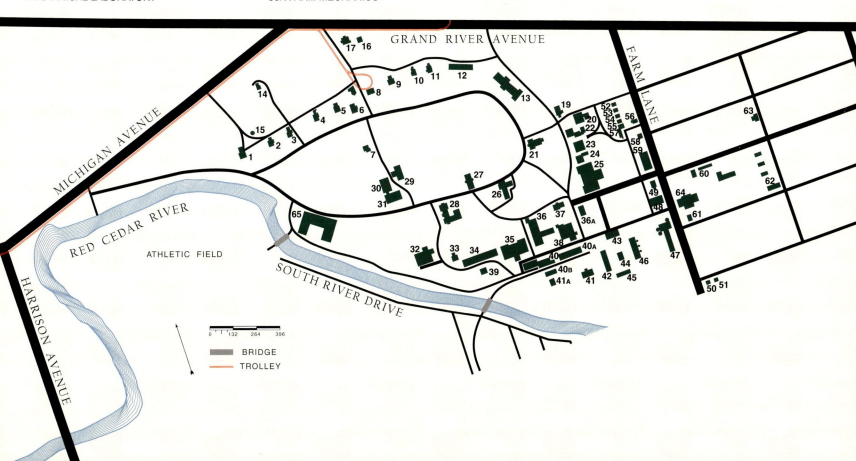

MICHIGAN AGRICULTURAL COLLEGE

CAMPUS LIFE 1900–1925

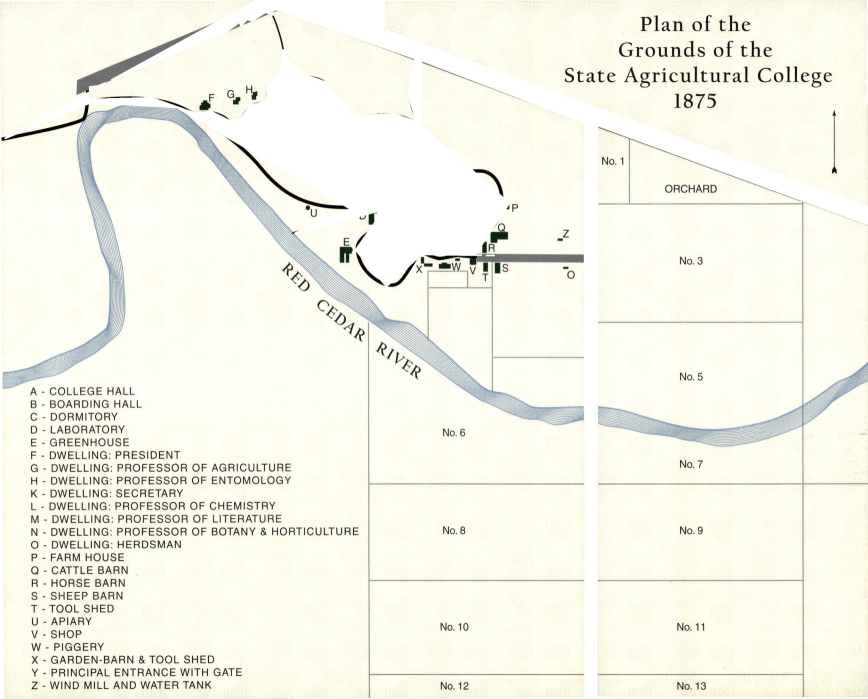

Plan of the
Grounds of the
State Agricultural College
1875

ORCHARD

No. 1

No. 3

No. 5

No. 6

No. 7

No. 8

No. 9

No. 10

No. 11

No. 12

No. 13

RED CEDAR RIVER

F G H

U

P

Q

Z

E

R

X W V T S

O

A - COLLEGE HALL
B - BOARDING HALL
C - DORMITORY
D - LABORATORY
E - GREENHOUSE
F - DWELLING: PRESIDENT
G - DWELLING: PROFESSOR OF AGRICULTURE
H - DWELLING: PROFESSOR OF ENTOMOLOGY
K - DWELLING: SECRETARY
L - DWELLING: PROFESSOR OF CHEMISTRY
M - DWELLING: PROFESSOR OF LITERATURE
N - DWELLING: PROFESSOR OF BOTANY & HORTICULTURE
O - DWELLING: HERDSMAN
P - FARM HOUSE
Q - CATTLE BARN
R - HORSE BARN
S - SHEEP BARN
T - TOOL SHED
U - APIARY
V - SHOP
W - PIGGERY
X - GARDEN-BARN & TOOL SHED
Y - PRINCIPAL ENTRANCE WITH GATE
Z - WIND MILL AND WATER TANK

MICHIGAN AGRICULTURAL COLLEGE

CAMPUS LIFE 1900–1925

a postcard tour

STEPHEN TERRY

Michigan Agricultural College Campus Life 1900 – 1925: A Postcard Tour
by Stephen Terry

Postcards presented herein from the collections of
Stephen Terry, Dennis Hansen, and Jeff Kacos.

Published by
Thunder Bay Press
Holt, Michigan

ISBN: 978-1-933272-44-3
Library of Congress Control Number: 2014948261

First Printing, First Edition
18   17   16   15   14   1   2   3   4   5

Book, Maps, and Cover Design by Julie Taylor
Printed in the United States of America

TABLE OF CONTENTS

DIRECTORY TO COLLEGE BUILDINGS

1913 CAMPUS MAP

1-7, 9-11, 14 RESIDENCES OF A PORTION OF
   THE FACULTY
8   EAST LANSING POST OFFICE
12 HOWARD TERRACE – RESIDENCE
13 WOMAN'S BUILDING – DORMITORY AND
   CLASS ROOMS
15 ASTRONOMICAL OBSERVATORY
16 COLLEGE HOSPITAL
17 U.S. WEATHER BUREAU
18 WAITING ROOM AND BOOK STORE
19 HORTICULTURAL LABORATORY
20 BACTERIOLOGICAL LABORATORY
21 LIBRARY AND MUSEUM – OFFICES OF THE
   PRESIDENT AND SECRETARY
22 BOTANICAL LABORATORY

23 FORESTRY BUILDING
24 ENTOMOLOGICAL LABORATORY
25 AGRICULTURAL BUILDING
26 WILLIAMS HALL – MEN'S DORMITORY
27 COLLEGE HALL
28 CHEMICAL LABORATORY
29 ABBOT HALL – MEN'S DORMITORY
30 BATHHOUSE
31 ARMORY
32 GREENHOUSE
33 UNION LITERARY SOCIETY BUILDING
34 WELLS HALL – MEN'S DORMITORY
35 ENGINEERING BUILDING
36 ENGINEERING SHOPS
36A FARM MECHANICS

37 VETERINARY LABORATORY
38 HEATING & LIGHTING PLANT
39 ASSAY LABORATORY
40 REPAIR SHOP & STORAGE
40A COAL STORAGE
40B STORAGE
41 HOG HOUSE
41A DETENTION BARN
42 SHEEP BARN
43 HORSE BARN
44 COMPOST SHED
45 BULL BARN
46 BEEF CATTLE BARN & SILOS
47 DAIRY BARN AND SILOS
48 IMPLEMENT BARN

49-51 FARM RESIDENCES
52-55 DETENTION HOSPITALS
56 RESIDENCE
57 HORTICULTURAL BARN
58 FRUIT HOUSE
59 DAIRY BUILDING
60 POULTRY PLANT
61 EXPERIMENT STATION BARN
62 BACTERIOLOGICAL STABLES
63 SOILS BUILDING
64 VETERINARY SURGERY & CLINIC
65 GYMNASIUM

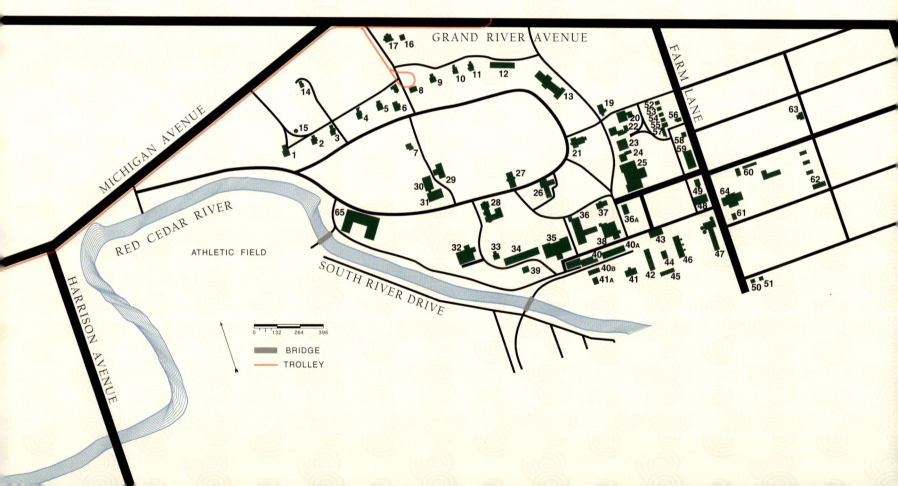

INTRODUCTION

Picture post cards came into popular usage at the beginning of the twentieth century. They quickly became a national craze, and the post card collecting hobby began. Publication of cards doubled every six months. By the year 1908, the US Post Office said that over 677 million cards were mailed at a time when the population of the country was only about 89 million people. The post card had become the e-mail, tweet, or text message medium of the times.

Early cards were printed primarily by German firms, who had the most advanced printing facilities of the time. Other cards, printed on photographic paper stock by local commercial photographers, were sold in the local stores. In 1906, Kodak introduced a folding camera with negatives of post card size, which could be printed on post card stock. Everyone could make their own post cards. These cards are one of a kind and are highly sought after by collectors. There are examples of them in this book.

The post card craze continued until 1918 when World War I destroyed the German printing industry and the expanding use of the telephone reduced the need for post cards as a method of keeping in touch. Today there is an active post card collecting market, but the early cards of the twentieth century are still the most prized.

With such a large supply to choose from, collectors began collecting only cards of special interest to themselves, a trend that has continued to the present day. Some collectors buy only cards from their home town, while others look for such topics as state capitols, train stations, ships or churches. And of course, many people collect cards from colleges or universities they attended. Such is the case here. The cards in this book are from the Michigan State collections of the author and two other collectors, Dennis Hansen and Jeffrey Kacos. The three of us have a common interest in MSU, having each spent long careers on the staff of the University.

The cards in this book are from a period of major development and growth for the small college on the Red Cedar. Enrollment grew from 652 in 1900 to 2,314 in 1925. The campus grew accordingly, as did the new city of East Lansing, which was incorporated in 1907.

This book presents a tour through the campus as it existed in the early 1900s. One entered the main campus entrance from Grand River at Evergreen Street. Trolley tracks coming from Lansing entered here. Most visitors to the campus in the early days of the twentieth century used the trolley to get to the campus. The trolley turned around on the campus in front of a trolley station which stood south of the present site of the Union Building. The main entrance was moved to Abbot Road in the 1920s.

The tour then makes a right turn along Faculty Row to the top of the hill, where the President's House stood. Then it generally follows the route of what is now West Circle Drive. Most of the area south of the river was used for agricultural purposes. Many barns and other farm buildings were found on north campus in the area where Farm Lane crosses the river. There were few buildings east of Farm Lane on north campus.

Our tour passes by the athletic fields on both sides of the river to the center part of the campus where the three original buildings stood. It passes Agriculture Hall and the older buildings of Laboratory Row and returns to its point of beginning, passing the Woman's Building and Howard Terrace, a faculty apartment building. While the general layout of this part of the campus has changed significantly since 1925, a review of the 1913 map will still look familiar to today's visitor. Only about a dozen of the buildings that existed in 1925 survive today.

While Agriculture was the prime focus of the college, expansion into Engineering and Veterinary Medicine took place in the early years and were an important part of the campus during the first part of the twentieth century. Our tour would not be complete without a closer look at these programs.

The Red Cedar River was an integral part of the campus from its very beginning, and scenes of the river and its bridges have long been favorites of collectors.

No tour of any campus would be complete without a look at the support activities of the campus. Yes, there are even postcards of smokestacks and steam tunnels.

The tour finishes at its point of beginning with a look at the single greatest event of the 1900-1925 period: the 1907 Semi-Centennial Celebration. President Theodore Roosevelt came to the campus to recognize the first half century of the nation's pioneer land grant college.

ENTRANCE TO THE CAMPUS M. A. C.

CAMPUS ENTRANCE

The main entrance to the campus was at the west end by Harrison Road for much of the nineteenth century, but in 1898 the trolley line was extended into the campus across from Evergreen Street and the main entrance to the campus shifted to near its present site at Abbot Road. The panoramic card shown on the previous page is a view of the campus from a site near the present Union Building.

Reached here at 1:30 last night. About 179 miles in the car, I surely enjoyed it. East Lansing is a beautiful city now I love it here. Tell all about my trip when I get home.

U. S. Weather Bureau, M. A. C.,
Lansing, Mich.

U.S. WEATHER BUREAU

U.S. WEATHER BUREAU

Weather observations and records are a critical need for an agricultural school. At MAC, these records were kept throughout its early history by Dr. R. C. Kedzie, Professor of Chemistry. From April 1863 until his death in 1902, Kedzie made and recorded detailed daily observations of weather conditions and reported them to the U. S. Weather Bureau. This work was continued by volunteers until 1910, when the U. S. Weather Bureau built this building on the campus. It was located at the main entrance to the campus adjacent to the trolley car loop. The building in the background was the campus hospital.

When the Weather Bureau withdrew from the campus, the building became the Music Building.

At this time the main entrance to the campus was located across from Evergreen Street. Abbot Road did not extend into the campus. This site eventually became the location of Campbell Hall.

7949 POST OFFICE M.A.C, EAST LANSING, MICH. PESHA PHOTO

POST OFFICE &

POST OFFICE & TROLLEY STATION

No. 2. Entrance to M.A.C. + Post Office East Lansing, Mich.

Until 1884, mail was delivered to the campus by a student who earned eight cents an hour to walk to Lansing and back with a twenty pound mail sack and assorted packages. Beginning in 1884, a US Post Office was established in the office of the Secretary of the Board in the Library and Museum (now Linton Hall). Mail was addressed to "Agricultural College, Michigan."

A trolley extended from Lansing in 1894 but stopped at Harrison Road by order of the State Board of Agriculture. They believed that extending it farther would bring in "undesirable elements" from Lansing and that it would make it easier for MAC students to find their way to Lansing saloons. A ride was a nickel, and passengers were expected to help put the car back on the tracks after

P.O. M.A.C.

frequent derailments. In 1898, the Board relented and the trolley line was extended into the campus, entering at a point across from Evergreen Street and ending in a loop near the present site of the Union Building. The trolley offered regular service except in the spring, when the rails were flooded between East Lansing and Lansing, and at Halloween, when student pranksters greased the tracks.

A Waiting Room and Post Office building was built at the end of the trolley loop. Trolleys arrived at fifteen-minute intervals. By 1913, the trolley line had been extended past the college entrance, turning north on MAC Avenue, then east again on Burcham, where it found its way to Pine Lake (now Lake Lansing). Eventually, the "interurban" tracks took passengers as far as Owosso. The entire system gave way to automobile traffic by 1929.

The Waiting Room was later expanded to provide room for a book store. The Post Office remained in the Waiting Room until the book store expanded into the space. The Post Office then moved into remodeled space in a frame Experiment Station building nearby. The mailing address became East Lansing upon incorporation of the city in 1907. Many early post cards carry the "Agricultural College" postmark.

UNION BUILDING

Interest in a student union began early in the twentieth century. Efforts to preserve College Hall, the first academic building on the campus, included a proposal that it be used as a site for a union for student use. The Class of 1915 promised a five dollar contribution from every member of the class if the alumni would begin a fund for a student union. In April of 1916 the MAC Union was organized at a mass meeting of the student body.

Following the collapse of College Hall in 1918, efforts turned to a new building. The end of the War provided a new catalyst to raise funds for a new building which would serve as a memorial to those who died in the War. Fund-raising efforts continued into the 1920s, but were never successful enough to pay the estimated $650,000 cost of a new building.

In 1923, ground was broken for the new building despite the lack of full funding. An "Excavation Week" was organized, and students, faculty, and alumni took turns working half day shifts with shovels to dig the foundation and basement by hand. An estimated 3,000 cubic yards of dirt was excavated. The cornerstone was laid in 1924 but work slowed to a halt as the private association ran out of money. The governor and the legislature stepped in, investing $300,000 of state money into the project, and the building was partially completed in time for the Sophomore Prom in 1925. The building included a ballroom, lounges, a cafeteria, soda shop, billiards room, barber and beauty shops, as well as hotel rooms for visiting alumni and parents on the upper floors.

Students paid $1.50 per term for membership in the Union. The college did not assume ownership of the building until 1936, when it secured federal funding to complete it.

View of Campus,
M. A. C.,
Lansing, Mich.

PRESIDENT'S HOUSE & FACULTY ROW

PRESIDENT'S HOUSE

uilt in 1857 and known today as Cowles House, the current home of MSU presidents is the oldest surviving building on the campus, though only parts of the original stone foundation and two exterior walls remain from the original structure. Linton Hall, built in 1881, is the oldest complete structure. The college's first president, Joseph R. Williams, lived in the President's House as did the third president, Theophilus C. Abbot.

But in 1873, this new residence was built for the president. Cowles House did not return to its use as a president's residence until 1941, when John A. Hannah moved in.

The 1873 house shown here was built at the end of Faculty Row, on the site currently occupied by Gilchrist Hall. College presidents and their families occupied it until the retirement of President Snyder in 1916. President Kedzie, who followed Snyder, lived in Lansing, and subsequent presidents lived in other houses on Faculty Row.

Following its use as the president's home, it became a women's dormitory until the mid-1920s, when it became the campus hospital. It was demolished following World War II to make room for Gilchrist Hall.

PRESIDENT'S HOUSE AT M. A. C., LANSING, MICH.

A Bit of the Campus at M. A. C., East Lansing, Mich.

First Snow 11/17/15

PIGS AND KIDS M.A.C.   C.E.W.

Lansing 5/31/07 Your Grand Pa

FACULTY ROW, M.A.C.   C.E.W.

Dear Sittie, — Cannot be certain but will probably be home next Monday or Tuesday. Am having a fine time. Wilfred.

Milford. June 7, '09.

Cannot be certain but will probably be home next Monday or Tuesday. Am having a fine time.

36. GYMNASIUM OF M. A. C., LANSING, MICH.

CAMPUS ATHLETICS

GYMNASIUM

The old Armory Building, built in 1885 when enrollment was 383 students, served for many years as the only venue for indoor physical training and athletics. By 1913, enrollment had grown to 1,534 and the old building was in constant demand. The MAC Record, the college weekly paper, noted in 1916 that "the poor old Armory is being worked overtime these days. The approach of cold weather drove the cadets indoors for drills, the basketball squad manages to secure the use of the floor for an hour or so a few times each week, and the evenings are occupied by the Dramatic Club, the Rifle Club or by a meeting of some sort. If the present rate of growth continues, open air meetings will become a popular necessity."

Gymnasium   Michigan State College   East Lansing

A new gymnasium was built nearby in 1918. The gymnasium, now known as IM Circle, included an indoor swimming pool, a large gym, and other athletic facilities. Shortly after it opened it became a temporary military barracks for a World War I Army training detachment during the Spanish influenza epidemic of 1918. It served both men and women students until 1940, when Jenison Field House was built. It then became known as the Women's Gym.

H. 1919

THE NEW GYM M.A.C. EAST LANSING MICH. No. 100

The building also became the home of the J Hop and other large gatherings, including commencement. Basketball was much more competitive here, as the old Armory had low steel roof beams that interfered with passing the ball, and the backboards were bolted directly to the end walls of the facility.

EL-6   GIRLS GYMNASIUM, MICHIGAN STATE COLLEGE, EAST LANSING, MICHIGAN
© Rex Photo

GYMNASIUM,
MICH. STATE COLLEGE.

GYMNASIUM, MICHIGAN STATE COLLEGE, EAST LANSING, MICHIGAN   EL502

ATHLETICS

Intercollegiate Athletics did not begin on the campus until 1884. The academic calendar of the time, almost unique in American higher education, ran through the summer from February through November and required fifteen hours of student labor and two periods of military drill each week in addition to the normal classroom load. This left little time for athletic pursuits.

Beginning in 1884, MAC participated in a series of field meets with Olivet and Albion Colleges. The addition of Hillsdale in 1887 resulted in the formation of the Michigan Inter-Collegiate Athletic Association (MIAA), which is now the nation's oldest athletic conference.

In 1896 the calendar was changed to a fall to spring format similar to most other institutions, and the mandatory student labor program was discontinued. These changes created much more time for students to pursue athletic activities.

Athletic Grounds, M. A. C., Lansing, Mich.

Increasing interest in athletics led to the purchase of 13 acres of low flood land south of the river. A wooden bridge was built from the north campus to the new field. A grandstand was built, followed by concrete bleachers nearby, to accommodate spectators at football, baseball, and track and field events. The Athletic Grounds continued to serve as the primary site for outdoor athletic events until 1923, when the MAC Stadium (now Spartan Stadium) was built. Now known as Old College Field, the area is still home to baseball, softball, and soccer programs.

Early records of MAC athletic competitions were lost in the Engineering Building fire of 1916, where they were kept in the office of Professor Herman Vedder, chair of the Athletic Council. The early history was laboriously reconstructed by Lyman Frimodig after he became a member of the Athletic Department staff. Frimodig was a student from 1914-1917 and set a record which still stands at MSU by winning 10 Varsity Letters in basketball, baseball, and football. His single game basketball scoring record of 30 points was not surpassed for 35 years. Frimodig spent over 41 years on the staff, serving many of them as the Business Manager. Frimodig's granddaughter, Peggy Brown, now holds the same position.

Following his retirement in 1960, Frimodig continued his hobby of maintaining records and other information about MSU's Intercollegiate Athletics history. In 1971 he co-authored a definitive history and records book *Spartan Saga: a History of Michigan State Athletics*.

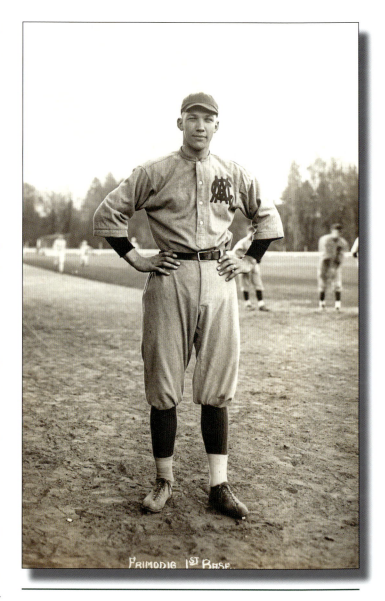

Lyman Frimodig, First Base

Varsity - M.A.C. - 1914.
— Harvey —

WABASH vs M.A.C.

C.E.W.

This shows our Ath. Field and the teams lined up as we kicked off to Wabash. Everything lovely here.

POST CARD

CORRESPONDENCE

NAME AND ADDRESS

Eva:-
Rec'd yours & J.B.
card all OK. Maybe
out after that cider
yet? This shows our
ath. field + the teams
lined up as we kicked-
off to wabash. x (me).
Everything lovely here.
Hear you go to Ypsi soon.
as ever ____

Miss Eva McCurdY
mason
mich.

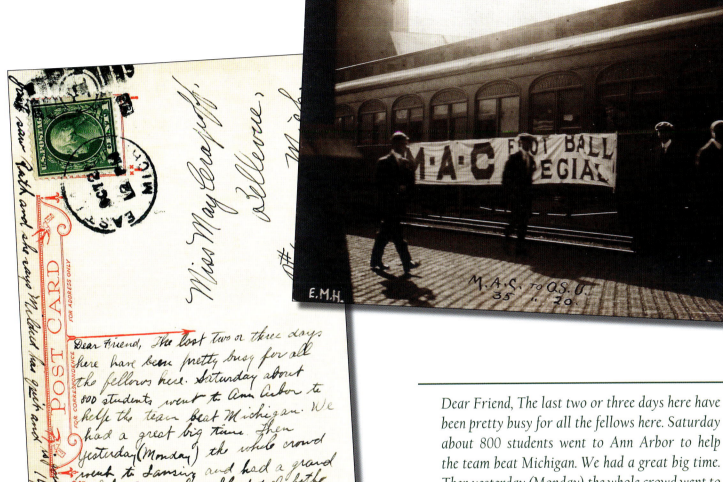

Dear Friend, The last two or three days here have been pretty busy for all the fellows here. Saturday about 800 students went to Ann Arbor to help the team beat Michigan. We had a great big time. Then yesterday (Monday) the whole crowd went to Lansing and had a grand celebration there. Lloyd and I both went down and helped yell.

MAC BAND

Today, all major colleges have bands. But in 1875, efforts to form the first student band at the college were hampered by the fact that there was only enough money for seven instruments. A band was formed and played for events on campus.

When the Military Department was formed in 1884, the first Cadet Band was organized. By 1913, the band had grown to 51. It included its first African-American member, a percussion player.

In 1907, the band created an embarrassing delay in the welcoming parade for President Roosevelt's speech at the Semi-Centennial celebration when four or five members went on strike, demanding to be paid for their effort. The remaining members of the band marched anyway. The two organizers of the strike were dismissed from school, and all the strikers were dismissed from the band. Beginning in 1908, the band had faculty leadership for the first time. A young chemistry professor, Arthur J. Clark, was assigned the responsibility.

Band -1913-

harvey 13

M.A.C. - 35
O.S.U. - 20.

M.A.C. BAND
SERENADING COLUMBUS, O.
F.M.H.

In 1912, the band made a road trip to Columbus, Ohio to play heavily favored Ohio State, a first-year member of the Big Ten. The Aggies, who had already been beaten by the University of Michigan by a 55-7 score, pulled off an amazing upset of the powerful Buckeyes, 35-20. The band paraded through the streets of Columbus and led a parade in Lansing to the Capitol. A Columbus paper said of the band "Never has there been a band on Ohio Field that can compare with the Michigan Aggie."

MAC FIELD

While intercollegiate football has been played on the campus since 1896, games prior to 1924 were played at Old College Field. Early teams were haphazardly organized and not very successful, with losing records in their first seven years. After losing to Michigan in 1902 at Ann Arbor by a score of 119-0, President Snyder commented, "If we must have football, I want the kind that wins." Chester Brewer was hired as coach, and for the next thirteen years, first under Brewer and later John F. Macklin, the Aggies had winning teams, including an undefeated season in 1913.

The football stadium was built in 1923 and dedicated during a game against Michigan in 1924 (the Aggies lost, 7-0). It seated 24,750 in concrete risers on the east and west, with additional seating in temporary bleachers in the end zones. It was originally named MAC Field, which was changed to Macklin Field in 1935. Additional seating was added in 1948, 1956, and 1957, when the name became Spartan Stadium.

Postcard manufacturers were not always good historians. This card lists the dedication as occurring at Michigan State College on 11/11/25. The actual event occurred on October 11, 1924, when the Michigan Agricultural College name was still in use.

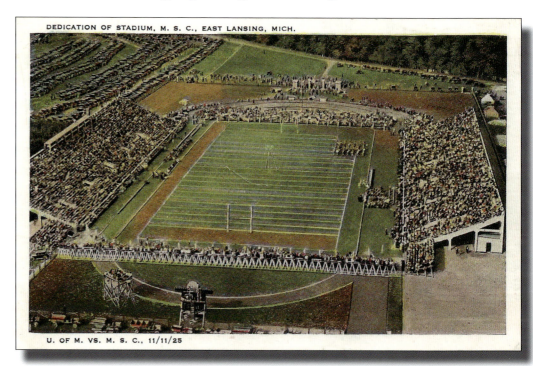

DEDICATION OF STADIUM, M. S. C., EAST LANSING, MICH.

U. OF M. VS. M. S. C., 11/11/25

CLASS RIVALRIES

Rowdiness among the student body had become a serious problem by the 1880s and 1890s. Freshmen were required to wear "beanies" throughout their entire freshman year and were easy targets for abuse by older students, especially sophomores. It was argued that expanding opportunities for women students would result in more civilized conduct of the almost exclusively male student body.

Class "Rushes" between the freshman and sophomore classes were common and became progressively more violent. Groups of students from one class would meet and challenge groups from the other class in what became shoving matches, fist fights, and efforts to throw others into the river or into the Class of '83 fountain.

Chester Brewer, Director of Physical Culture (and highly successful football coach) helped to resolve the problem by organizing an annual event between the two classes. Events included wrestling, a canvas pull, football scrambles, a tug of war across the Red Cedar, and a "flag-rush"

THE GAME LOSERS TUG OF WAR 1915

where each class tried to capture the flag of the other. Points were awarded and classes competed to see who could become the overall winner. Posters deriding the opposing class were posted throughout the campus. Large crowds gathered for these contests, and the entire event became a major focal point of the campus social year.

The rushes, though organized, continued to be very physical. Writing home in 1910, one student said to a friend, "You ought to have been here and helped us poor freshies in our class fight. We had a great time but I came out alright. Some got hurt pretty bad. The sophs gave our tug-a-war men a swim across the river. They didn't get our banner off the tree."

Beginning in 1908, the new Student Council was formed to set rules of conduct regarding class rivalries. Hazing was prohibited, smoking on campus was banned, and a formal "Cap Night" was organized. A bonfire was set in Sleepy Hollow, east of the present Music Building, and freshmen threw their caps into the fire.

FLAG FIGHT

CANVAS PULL

FOOT BALL RUSH M.A.C. OCT. 1H9

Also in 1908 the sophomores invited the freshmen to a Barbecue on the lawn in front of Wells Hall, then located on the site of the current Library. The sophomore class president presented a carving knife to the freshman president, and a truce was declared. A tradition was born and by 1915, the Barbecue event involved a major bonfire.

Not all problems of rowdiness were eliminated by the formal rivalries, though. Student Don Waldron in a November 1919 post card wrote, "I have had a few rather exciting experiences including being shoved through a bridge rail and being dropped 10 ft onto a log in the river. A big bunch of them went off (the bridge) and I was buried in the river bottom. I was lucky, quite a few were badly hurt."

Class rushes continued to be a focal point of the year throughout the 1920s.

Photo, Only, Copyright 1906 by the Rotograph Co
Armory, Lansing, Mich.

ARMORY BUILDING &
WARTIME ON CAMPUS

THE ARMORY

While the college's land grant status required military training for all able-bodied students, actual military training was haphazard and erratic until 1885, when a regular army lieutenant was detailed to the campus in response to a petition signed by almost every student. By the fall of 1886, a new armory was available for use. It was located on the site of the present Music Building. A drill field was cleared to the west of the building across from Faculty Row. Participation in military training was voluntary until becoming mandatory in 1888 for all male students except seniors. There were very few female students at this time.

While it was deemed satisfactory for military purposes, the Armory had shortcomings with respect to its other intended uses as a gymnasium and for lectures. The tar and gravel floor had a disagreeable odor, and the building was not equipped with any athletic equipment. After a few years, a maple floor was installed and athletic equipment acquired.

THE ARMORY M.A.C.   EAST LANSING, MICH.

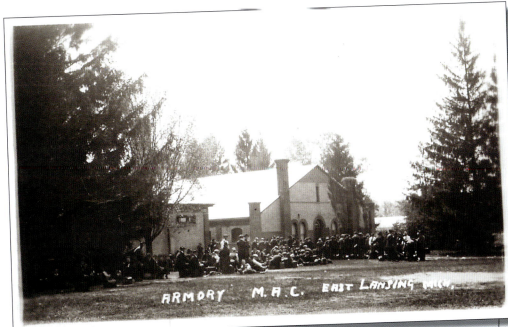

ARMORY   M.A.C.   EAST LANSING, MICH.

Hello Mother, here we are as we lined up to be recorded. My squad is in the center to the right standing in line, the morning we arrived, are having fine weather here, although awfully cold nights. We have shower baths and swimming tanks in the building on the left, and athlete field on this side, still under quarantine. Maybe for a week yet. Could you send me the Barron paper when you can. So long, A.W.D., E.L. Mich.

In 1904 a new bath house with a small pool was added to the Armory. The bath house replaced an older one built in 1888. The original bath house had only 10 zinc bathtubs. In good weather, students grew tired of waiting in line to use the bathtubs and bathed in the river instead.

Weekly parades on the drill field were conducted with the men marching to the music of the cadet band. In addition, military training included drills and "sham battles" between the companies of student soldiers.

DRILL GROUND. M.A.C.

WARTIME ON CAMPUS

When war was declared in the spring of 1917, senior men who enlisted in the Officers Training Camp were awarded their diplomas early. Similarly, juniors who enlisted were awarded credit for spring term work. This echoed the actions of the Civil War over fifty years earlier, when the entire seven-man graduating class of 1861 left early and enlisted in the Army. They were granted their diplomas in absentia.

An Army Training Detachment of 500 men was assigned to the campus in May of 1918. Five temporary barracks buildings and two mess halls, one of which is shown here, were constructed on the present site of Berkey Hall. The male student body declined so sharply that Abbot Hall was closed and the other dormitories had empty rooms. Another detachment of 500 men who met the requirements to be college students arrived. They lived in Abbot Hall and the other two men's dormitories, as well as on the top floors of Agriculture Hall and Olds Hall.

Soldier Leo Coohon of Sturgis wrote home on September 30, 1919, "This is sure some great place. We can't go off the campus yet for another week. We're some busy too I'll tell you."

All of this activity was interrupted in mid-October when the great Spanish influenza epidemic of 1918 broke out among the recruits. The uninfected soldiers were moved to the new Gymnasium and the barracks were used as quarantine wards for the infected. Women students were kept apart from the soldiers and wore masks to and from class. A total of eighteen men, including one faculty member, died in the epidemic. Hundreds of others fell ill.

In all, a total of forty-nine men of MAC lost their lives in World War I.

Hello! How's the boy anyhow? I'm all O.K. This is sure some great place. How's Leo P? Tell him he ought to be here. We can't go off the campus yet for another week. We're some busy too I'll tell you.

Co. F. 1914.

Co. H. Prize Company 1914.

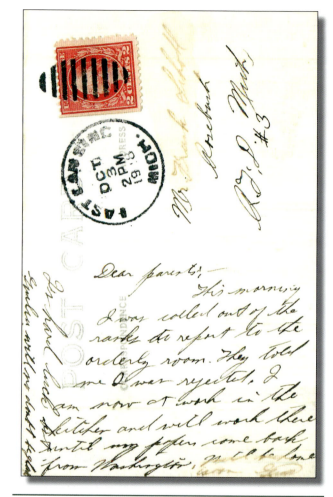

Dear Parents: This morning I was called out of the ranks to report to the orderly room. They told me I was rejected. I am now at work in the kitchen and will work there until my papers come back from Washington. Is hard luck but G— will no doubt be glad. Will be home soon.

CAMPUS GARDENS
& ARBORETUM

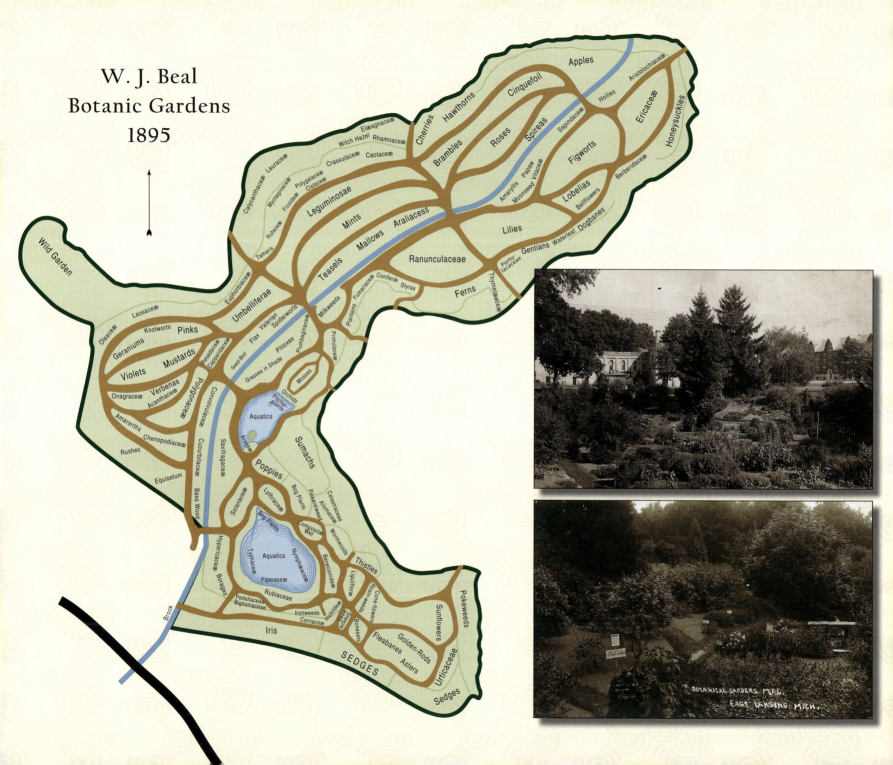

W. J. Beal
Botanic Gardens
1895

Wild Garden

Cherries
Hawthorns
Cinquefoil
Apples
Aristolochiaceae
Hollies
Roses
Spireas
Ericaceae
Honeysuckles
Brambles
Sapindaceae
Figworts
Berberidaceae
Elæagnaceæ
Witch Hazel Rhamnaceæ
Crassulaceæ Caotaceæ
Amaryllis Papaw
Moonseed Vitaceæ
Lobelias
Bellflowers
Calycanthaceæ Lauraceæ
Myrsinaceæ
Polygalaceæ
Ficoideæ Cistaceæ
Leguminosae
Rutaceæ
Lilies
Mints
Araliacess
Dogbanes
Gentians Waterleaf
Tamarix
Mallows
Ranunculaceae
Thymelæaceæ
Portu-
lacaceæ
Teasels
Euphorbiaceæ
Ferns
Umbelliferae
Milkweeds
Plantains Fumariaceæ Coniferæ Styrax
Laosaceæ
Pinks
Flax Valerian Spiderworts
Oleaceæ
Knotworts
Phloxes
Plumbaginaceæ
Geraniums
Reseedaceæ
Seed-Bed
Grasses in Shade
Primulaceæ
Violets
Mustards
Cappardaceæ
Mosses
Onagraceæ
Verbenas
Acanthaceæ
Orchids
Pitcher Plants
Amaranths
Chenopodiaceæ
Polygonaceæ
Convolvulaceæ
Aquatics
Araceæ
Sumachs
Rushes
Saxifragaceæ
Cucurbitaceæ
Poppies
Equisetum
Bass Wood
Solanaceæ
Lythraceæ
Bog Plants
Pickereweed
Celastraceæ
Alismaceæ
Hypericaceæ
Bog Plants
Typhaceæ
Compositæ
Wet
Wormwoods
Thistles
Borages
Aquatics
Nymphaceæ
Beneloideæ
Piperaceæ
Liguliflora
Pedaliaceæ
Bignoniaceæ
Rubiaceæ
Resinweeds
Cone-flowers
Pokeweeds
Ironweeds
Inuloideæ
Bonesets
Sunflowers
Cornaceæ
Golden-Rods
Iris
Fleabanes
Asters
Urticaceæ
SEDGES
Sedges
Brook

BOTANICAL GARDENS M.A.C.
EAST LANSING MICH.

CAMPUS GARDENS

Almost from the outset, early faculty members sought to develop campus gardens as tools for student instruction and to demonstrate the value of the college to the agricultural community of the state. This process was aided by the college policy of requiring three hours of labor per day from each student. Faculty believed that the labor requirement helped to make students proficient in new agricultural techniques and encouraged them to return to farming after graduation. Students were paid up to eight cents per hour for the labor, which helped to defray costs of attending.

The labor requirement was dropped in 1896, but the effort of those early students and faculty had produced a campus that was widely known for its natural beauty, and their gardens were maintained and expanded throughout the early 1900s as well. Horticultural gardens stretched to the east from the Woman's Building (which became the original Morrill Hall) all the way to Bogue Street. The MSU of today continues to honor its history through the preservation of the Beal Gardens, which are the longest continuously operated botanical gardens in the nation. New Horticultural Demonstration Gardens were created on south campus in 1987 when the Plant and Soil Science Building was being built.

Botanic Garden, M. A. C., Lansing, Mich.

Botanical Gardens at State College

Horticultural Gardens. M.A.C. East Lansing Mich. MI201

Log Cabin at M.A.C. East Lansing Mich. M1224

Wild Garden - M.A.C. No.9

GREENHOUSE

This 1913 building stood on the bank of a ravine near the Red Cedar River. It is the second greenhouse on this site and was the primary laboratory of Professor W. J. Beal, who served for forty years on the faculty of the college (1870-1910).

In the ravine next to the greenhouse, between the Gymnasium and what is now the Library, Beal planted a botanical "wild garden" as an educational tool for his students. He selected the site because he believed it to be unsuitable for building construction and would thus survive for many years as a botanical teaching and research tool. His garden was expanded continually throughout his tenure and grew into one of the finest botanical gardens in the country.

Today, the greenhouse is gone, replaced by the Library, but the Beal Botanical Gardens still survive as a tribute to this pioneering teacher.

FlowerBeds-M.A.C.

Dear Matie, Just to let you know I arrived here O.K. The ground outside doesn't look like this in the picture. For there is snow all over. It started to snow last night when we were about half way up here.

ARBORETUM & LOVERS LANE

Beginning about 1875, Professor William J. Beal began planting an arboretum at the intersection of what is now Grand River and Michigan Avenue adjacent to what was then the north entrance to the campus. Over the years he planted an estimated 215 varieties of plants and shrubs on a 1½ acre plot of land. The site was deliberately selected because of its visibility to passengers on the trolley and interurban cars that passed by on the adjacent tracks on the way from Lansing to the campus, to Pine Lake (now Lake Lansing), and on to Owosso. A Deer Park was developed nearby in about 1898.

Arboretum, M. A. C., Lansing, Mich.

LOVERS LANE. LANSING MICH.

Students on their way to and from East Lansing created pathways through the arboretum, and one in particular became known as Lovers Lane. The popular post card scene centered above, postmarked in 1908, shows two people on the path. The people were probably added by the publisher to provide interest, as this same publisher used very similar characters in other views elsewhere on and off the campus. This was a fairly common practice at the time.

THE WILLOWS

At one time a small gully ran to the south through the center of the campus, from near the present site of the Union Building to Sleepy Hollow. A rustic bridge spanned the ravine through a clump of willow trees on a walk between the Trolley Station and the Library. The scene became a popular one for postcards regardless of the season. The gully was eventually filled in, but the willows were still standing at the time of the Centennial celebration in 1955.

THE WILLOWS, M. A. C.   EAST LANSING, MICH.

The Willows in Winter, M. A. C., Lansing, Mich.

DEER PARK

Deer Park was created in 1898 on about two acres of land, including part of the Arboretum, near the intersection of Grand River and Michigan Avenue. Two elk and a family of three deer were obtained from Belle Isle Park in Detroit. The park was not very successful. The elk killed one of the deer and had to be segregated and ultimately sold. The deer experienced bad health and the herd gradually shrank to three.

Still, the park was popular with visitors to the campus until it was closed after a fairly short existence.

Copyright 1904 by the Rotograph Co.

G 3799 Abbott Hall, Agricultural College, Lansing, Mich.

ABBOT HALL

ABBOT HALL

Constructed in 1888 to house male students, the first Abbot Hall was modified to accommodate the new women's "domestic economy" program in 1896. Newest of the three dormitory buildings at the time, it housed forty women, who learned practical skills in a sewing room and cooking laboratory on the second floor of an addition to the building. It served as the home of the women's program until the new Woman's Building (later known as Morrill Hall) was constructed in 1900.

Over time, the building also became known as the Campus Inn. In 1918 Pvt. Clarence Spink, on campus for World War I military training, wrote home, "Well, Ben, this is the life. We eat in this building and sleep in the Armory. Regular work doesn't start until Monday."

The Abbot Hall name was assigned to the new Mason-Abbot Hall in 1938, and the old building became the Music Practice Building, a suitable use because its masonry construction provided much more noise control than the frame-structure buildings which preceded it. It was demolished and replaced by the current Music Practice Building in 1968.

ABBOT HALL AND THE COLLEGE INN, MAC, EAST LANSING, MICH. 11-96

Abbott Hall and Armory, M. A. C.
East Lansing, Mich.

Well, Ben, this is the life. We eat in this building and sleep in the Armory. Regular work doesn't start until Monday.

Abbot Hall.
M.A.C.
E. Lansing, Mich.
10371.

IVY COVERED ABBOTT,
MICH. STATE COLLEGE,

7943 CHEMIS... BUILDING. M.A.C. E LANSING, MICH. PESKA PHOTO

CHEMISTRY BUILDING

CHEMISTRY

An appropriation of $10,000 in 1869 built a new Chemistry Laboratory. Popularly known as the "Chem Fort" because of its flat roof and imposing front appearance, the building survived well into the twentieth century. It was located near the present site of the Library.

All students were required to take chemistry, so as the enrollment grew, so did the Chem Fort. A three story addition in 1911 contained a lecture room seating 250. In his semi-centennial history of the college, Professor W. J. Beal notes that the lecture hall was, "alas, too small in the fall of 1913!" Total enrollment that fall was 1,534.

Photo. Only, Copyright 1904 by the Rotograph Co.
Chemical Laboratory, Agricultural College, Lansing, Mich.

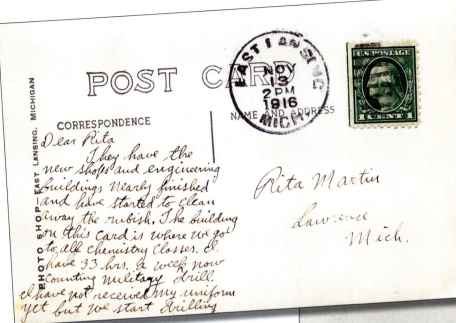

POST CARD

EAST LANSING, MICHIGAN

CORRESPONDENCE

PHOTO SHOP, EAST LANSING. MICHIGAN

Dear Rita
They have the new shops and engineering buildings nearly finished and have started to clean away the rubish. The building on this card is where we go to all chemistry classes. I have 33 hrs. a week now counting military drill. I have not received my uniform yet but we start drilling

NAME AND ADDRESS

EAST LANSING MICH
NOV 13 2PM 1916

Rita Martin

Lawrence

Mich.

Dear Rita, They have the new shops and engineering buildings nearly finished and have started to clean away the rubbish. The building on this card is where we go to all chemistry classes. I have 33 hours a week now counting military drill. I have not received my uniform yet but we start drilling.

7867 CHEMICAL LABORATORY, MAC, LANSING MICH — PESHA PHOTO

Chemistry Bldg. M.A.C. No.18

College Hall, M. A. C.
East Lansing, Mich.

COLLEGE HALL

COLLEGE HALL

College Hall was the first building in America dedicated to the teaching of scientific agriculture. It was originally conceived as a large building with a central hall and two wings, but lack of funding limited construction to a 50 by 100 foot west wing. It housed all laboratory, classroom, and office space of the new college.

To the east of this building stood the only other completed building on the campus of the new college. Known as "Saint's Rest," it was a boarding hall for students. It burned in 1876.

Bricks for College Hall were made on-site and just to the west of the building. The resulting depression in the ground survives to this day and is known as Sleepy Hollow, located east of the present Music Building. Poorly constructed, the building had a leaky roof which caused plaster to fall for years after its opening. Doors would not close and the floors were uneven. Portions of the foundation were laid on planks, which eventually rotted, and a corner of the

COLLEGE HALL, M.A.C.

College Hall, M. A. C.   EAST LANSING, Mich.

foundation included an old tree stump. Administration of the entrance exam for the first class of students was delayed for a month because the contractor would not release control of the building until he was paid, and the state would not release payment until some of the structural defects were corrected.

In an era when natural light provided the most useful source of illumination, the building was notable for its lack of windows. Faculty complained endlessly about the poor lighting conditions in the building, and corner rooms were highly prized.

Despite efforts to preserve it, in August of 1918 two walls of the building collapsed during a war trainees' retreat while the band played the national anthem in front of it. Today's band still claims credit for the collapse.

The rest of the building did not die easily, however. As late as 1928, part of the foundation was still in use as an artillery garage.

John W. Beaumont, a member of the State Board of Agriculture from 1912 to 1921, had assumed responsibility for directing the efforts to renovate College Hall. Following the collapse of the building, he offered to build a bell tower as a gift to commemorate the Hall. Today, Beaumont Tower stands on the site of MAC's first building.

College Hall, Williams Hall & Chemical Laboratory, M.A.C. E. Lansing, Mich. 10378

Post Card

Well Frank I suppose you are still going to Rankletown school you had ought to be out here haveing one — of a time This is way ahead of Rankin in every way. A. G.

Mr. Frank Pierce
Linden
Mich.
R. #1.

NOV 14 1910 EAST LANSING MICH

Well, Frank, I suppose you are still going to Rankletown school. You had ought to be out here having one — of a time. This is way ahead of Rankin in every way. A. G.

WILLIAMS HALL, M. A. C., LANSING, MICH.

WILLIAMS HALL

WILLIAMS HALL

The second dormitory built on campus, Williams Hall was built in 1869 to provide additional housing for expansion of the student body. In the late 1860s, as many as half of new applicants to the college were rejected due to lack of housing. The building was named in honor of Joseph R. Williams, the college's first president. The building was located on the site of the current MSU Museum. In addition to housing 80 students, the YMCA was housed on the first floor of the building along with some guest rooms. The basement also served as the dining hall for the entire student body. The tower housed the campus bell, used for many years to mark the events of the day, from wake up at 5:30 AM throughout the day until dinner.

Appropriations for the hall by the Legislature were significant for another reason: they ended an ongoing effort led by farm interests in southeast Michigan and at the University of Michigan to close the new agricultural college and to transfer its activities and its Morrill Act Land Grant endowments to the University of Michigan.

Williams Hall. M.A.C.

Williams Hall, Agricultural College, Lansing, Mich.

Y.M.C.A., East Lansing, Mich. 68124.

The building burned down on January 1, 1919. It was largely vacant at the time, as the World War I army activities had ended and students had not moved back in. Loss of the space accelerated the move of students to off campus housing, as only Wells Hall remained for men.

The current Williams Hall, in the West Circle group of residence halls, is named for President William's wife, Sarah Langdon Williams. When the dormitory steward resigned in 1858, Mrs. Williams stepped in and helped students prepare and serve meals for the remaining four months of the term.

Library and Museum, M. A. C.,
Lansing, Mich.

LIBRARY & MUSEUM

LIBRARY & MUSEUM

Built in 1881 to house the museum and library, this building was also the administration building until the late 1960s. The tower of the Victorian-styled building faces the center of the campus, away from the current West Circle Drive. The original main campus road passed in front of this tower. The President's Office was located in the building from its opening in 1881 until 1969, with the exception of a few years when it was located in the new library (now the MSU Museum). A large addition facing West Circle Drive was constructed in 1947.

Now known as Linton Hall, the building is generally recognized as the oldest surviving building on the campus. Cowles House, the President's residence, was originally built in 1857, but subsequent expansions have left only the original fieldstone foundation and two walls visible to the passerby.

Library, Agricultural College, Lansing, Mich.

Museum & Library M.A.C. East Lansing Mich.

M.A.C. Library & Museum. Lansing, Mich.

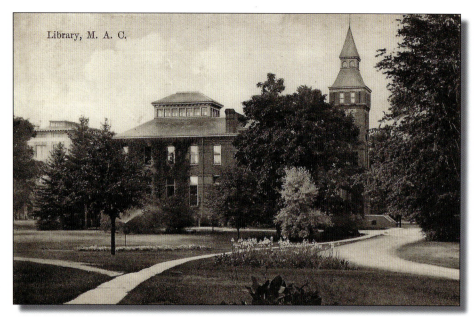

Library, M. A. C.

Library & Museum, M.A.C. E. Lansing, Mich.

Library M.A.C.

Womens Building, Michigan Agricultural College, Lansing, Mich.

WOMAN'S BUILDING

WOMAN'S BUILDING

The first women were admitted to MAC in 1870. They took the same farming curriculum as the men, though they did not participate in the three hours of farm labor required of male students five days each week. Since male students were given preference in admissions, enrollment of women remained low for many years. Due to the isolation of the campus from Lansing, off campus housing was not available, and special arrangements had to be made for women students.

In 1896, the first program specifically for women was created, and the Home Economics Department was organized. The Woman's Building opened in 1900 with housing space for 120 women. Additional facilities in the building included offices, classrooms, a cooking laboratory, music rooms, and sitting rooms. Known as "The Coop" (because it was where the hens lived), the building served as the primary housing facility for women until 1931, when Mayo Hall, the first West Circle building, was constructed.

Women's Bldg, M.A.C., East Lansing, Mich.

G8114

WOMAN'S BUILDING

Funds ran short during construction of the Woman's Building, and a planned west wing of the building was not constructed, giving the finished building a somewhat lopsided appearance. Trees were planted around the west end of the building to hide the asymmetry.

In 1937, the building was remodeled into classroom, laboratory, and office space for academic departments and renamed Morrill Hall in recognition of Justin Morrill, author of the original Morrill Act which created the land grant colleges. This building survived until 2013, when its deteriorated condition resulted in its demolition. In ongoing recognition of Morrill, Agriculture Hall was renamed the Morrill Hall of Agriculture.

An estimated 75% of the building was saved and recycled into other uses. The landscaped plaza that stands on the site today includes materials from the building.

WOMEN'S BUILDING M.A.C.
EAST LANSING, MICH.

In the hall of the Ladies Building
Ray

PARLOR WOMEN'S BUILDING.   M.A.C.

East Lansing, Mich.
April 4, 1916

Dear Matie,

Arrived here O.K. about
12:00 o'clock. Registered and
paid my fees. I have a class
the last hour Friday so
when I come home my folks
will have to meet me in
Jackson. There is a new
Moving Picture Show started
up out here now. Start to
classes in the morning.

Sereno

Miss Matie Dancer,

Horton,

Mich.

Arrived here O.K. about 12:00 o'clock.
Registered and paid my fees. I have a
class the last hour Friday, so when I
come home my folks will have to meet
me in Jackson. There is a new Moving
Pictures Show started up out here now.
Start to classes in the morning.

"WINTER SCENE" M.A.C. M.W

BIRD'S EYE VIEW OF HOWARD TERRACE AND WOMANS BLDG. M.A.C. No.19

Copyright 1904 by the Retograph Co.

G 3804 Howard Terrace, Agricultural College, Lansing, Mich.

HOWARD TERRACE &
HOME ECONOMICS

HOWARD TERRACE

In the early years, when the campus was located in a wilderness, housing had to be provided for all faculty. Howard Terrace was built in 1888 for this purpose. Located near the site of the present Human Ecology Building, it contained eight apartments for faculty assistants with families. Professors were provided homes on Faculty Row, where the West Circle Residence Halls now stand. Single faculty assistants, all male in those years, were housed in Station Terrace, a frame building to the west of Howard Terrace.

By 1912, growing needs for housing for the expanded women's program required placement of women students in the building, and beginning in 1914 it housed only women students.

The building was demolished in 1922, in preparation for the construction of a new Home Economics Building.

HOME ECONOMICS

HOME ECONOMICS BUILDING, M. S. C., EAST LANSING, MICH.

Continued growth in the women's program led to construction of the Home Economics building, completed in 1924. The building was constructed on the former site of Howard Terrace, a faculty apartment and then a women's dormitory, next to the Woman's Building built in 1900. All instructional activities were transferred to this building from the Woman's Building, though women students continued to live in the Woman's Building until the West Circle residence halls were built in the 1930s.

Home Economics and Horticulture were the only academic buildings constructed on the campus during the period of rapid expansion between 1914 and 1925.

The building is known today as Human Ecology.

4736—HOME ECONOMICS, MICH. AGRICULTURAL COLLEGE, LANSING, MICH.

G 3816 Wells Hall, Agricultural College, Lansing, Mich.

WELLS HALL

WELLS HALL

The Wells Hall of today, located south of the river and east of the stadium, is the third campus building to carry the name. The first, an imposing brick building, was a boarding hall on the campus. It housed 128 students and replaced Saints Rest, the first hall, which burned in 1876. The building was named after Judge Hezekiah Wells, who was president of the State Board of Agriculture (the college's governing body) for most of the first 22 years of its existence. It was located near the river and close to the present site of the Library.

The first Wells Hall burned in 1905 and was replaced by the second one in 1907. Located near the original Wells, it was divided into six "wards", each with its own entrance and separated by masonry walls to protect against fires. The arrangement also helped to control noise

7814. WELLS HALL, MICHIGAN AGRICULTURAL. COLLEGE.　　　DETROIT PUBLISHING CO.

A 3816 Wells Hall, Agricultural College, Lansing, Mich.

Wells Hall, Union Lit. Bldg., Agricultural College, Lansing, Mich.

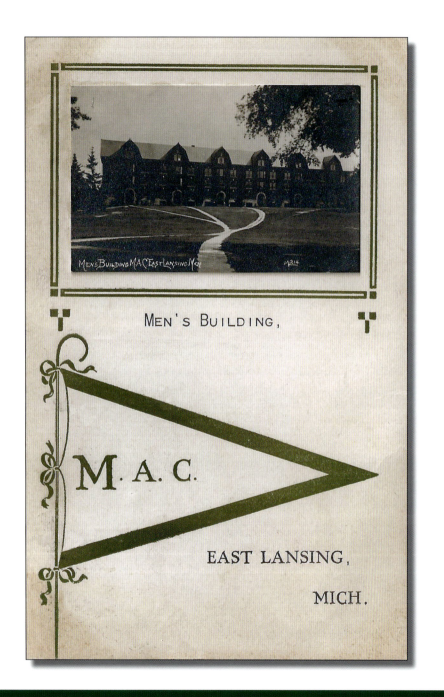

MEN'S BUILDING,

M.A.C.

EAST LANSING,

MICH.

from student rooms, a common problem in the wood-frame structures of the day. The building suffered fire damage when the adjacent engineering building burned in 1916, but was saved and repaired. It survived until 1966, though not as student housing. Wells Hall was demolished to provide space for the east wing of the library.

Both Wells Halls and the Woman's Building (later known as Morrill Hall), were the subject of many post cards, as students wanted family and friends back home to see what their living environments were like.

Dear Miss C. — Hope you had a good time at the "Creek." Had an Auto ride out to College and viewed this building.

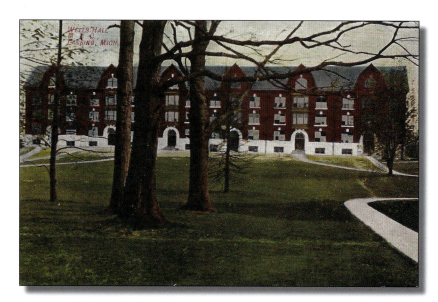

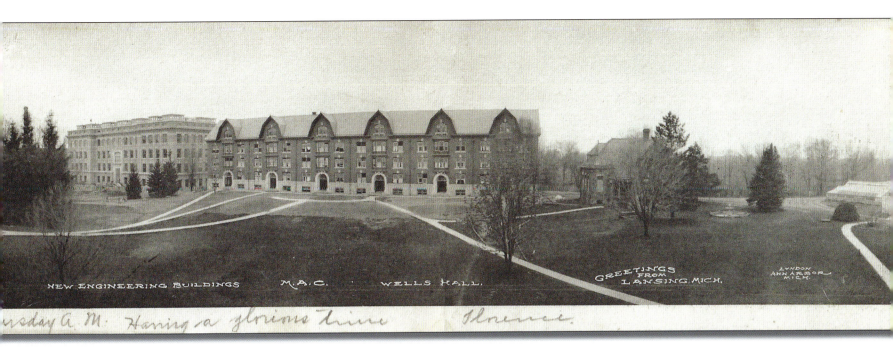

NEW ENGINEERING BUILDINGS.   M.A.C.   WELLS HALL.   GREETINGS FROM LANSING, MICH.   LYNDON ANN ARBOR MICH.

Thursday A.M. Having a glorious time.
Florence

Wells Hall
Michigan State College
East Lansing

NO. 3   WELLS HALL & ENGINEERING BLDG.

Hello Herman— I thought I'd drop you a card and let you know how I'm getting along. I'm alright excepting that I got a shot in the arm yesterday that is a dose of inoculation, which makes my arm kind of sore. The big building on the other side is where we get our meals in the basement. The other is the R.E. Olds Hall of Engineering.

Old Engineering Bldg. M.A.C. Lansing, Mich.

ENGINEERING BUILDING

ENGINEERING BUILDINGS

Offering instruction in the "branches of learning... related to the mechanical arts" was required under the terms of the Morrill Act of 1862, which established the Land Grant schools and funded them through grants of Federal land. MAC, established in 1855, was the prototype for this legislation. The law provided for the granting of 250,000 acres of Federal land to the state, the sale of which provided most of the funding for the new agricultural school for many years.

Yet it was not until 1885 that an engineering program was initiated by the college, in the face of opposition from the farming community and the University of Michigan engineering program. An appropriation of $17,000 from the Michigan Legislature provided funding for a new building, a faculty residence, and annual salary for a professor of mechanics.

The new program attracted an initial class of forty-three students, of which only six graduated. In addition to classroom work, students were required to spend five afternoons a week in the new shops, learning practical applications in woodworking, metal work, and foundry skills, among others. With faculty supervision, students made many of the tools used in the shops. They spent time on Saturday mornings doing projects of personal interest, including folding beds for their own use and those of friends in the dormitories.

BURNING M.A.C. SHOPS AND ENGINEERING BLDG.

ENGINEERING BLDG M.A.C. BURNS
MAR. 5th 1916
HARV.

MESSAGE

ADDRESS

Dear Aunt and Uncle and
Cousins:
The picture on the other
side of this is of the building which
burned last Sunday
morning. Our High School burned
to the ground Sunday night and
now we have to hold school in
the church out here. Hope you
people are all well.
Arthur D.

Mr. & Mrs. Fred Bluemly

R. F. D. No 5

Iowa.
Mich

Dear Aunt and Uncle and Cousins: The picture on the other side of this is of the building which burned last Sunday morning. Our High School burned to the ground Sunday night and now we have to hold school in the church out here. Hope you people are all well. Arthur D.

The original building, constructed in the 1880s, was supplemented by a large new Engineering Hall in 1907.

The entire engineering complex burned on Sunday, March 5, 1916, with collateral damage to the roof and attic rooms of Wells Hall to the west. While Wells was restored, the engineering buildings were a complete loss. A student wrote, "I suppose you saw in the Detroit paper about the fire. I did not hear about it until I reached Lansing. Then coming out to East Lansing on the car we saw another blaze start. It was the East Lansing High School. It burned to the ground. The Engineering Building, Forge Shop and Machine Shops are all burnt up."

The fire also rekindled the ongoing controversy concerning whether MAC should have an engineering program at all. Editorials were written and lobbying efforts in the Legislature were begun to block appropriations for new buildings and to close the program and transfer it to the University of Michigan. Fearing

North-east Corner of Eng. Shops. Mar. 5, 1916. "Big"

South-east Corner, Eng. Bldg. 3/5/16. "Big"

Mechanical Engineering Building, M. A. C., Lansing, Mich.

that the Legislature would agree, President Kedzie contacted Ransom E. Olds with a request for help. Olds responded with a gift of $100,000. When combined with available land grant funds, the gift was enough to reconstruct the Engineering Hall and three shops. The resulting building, renamed Olds Hall, was virtually an exact replica of the structure it replaced. While no longer used for engineering, it continues to provide space for a number of university departments.

ONE OF THE NEW SHOPS
M. A. C.

OLDS HALL OF ENGINEERING
MICH. STATE COLLEGE.

Engineering Building M.A.C.

C.E.W.   BIRD'S EYE VIEW M.A.C.

AGRICULTURE

LABORATORY ROW

A series of five laboratory buildings were built between 1889 and 1902, east of the Library and Museum Building (now Linton Hall), on a road that eventually became part of West Circle Drive. At the time of their construction, the main road ran on the west side of the Library and Museum.

These buildings survive intact today but are no longer laboratory buildings. They were originally occupied by departments in the agriculture program, including dairy, botany, bacteriology, and horticulture. Over their original lifetimes as laboratory buildings, they also housed programs in forestry and entomology. Today they have been preserved and serve academic programs not directly associated with their original purposes. They are known as Laboratory Row in recognition of their original purpose, and the entire group is listed on the State Register of Historic Sites. Their current names and original purposes are (from north to south) Eustace-Cole Hall (Horticulture), Marshall Hall (Bacteriology), Old Botany (Botany), Chittenden Hall (Dairy), and Cook Hall (Agriculture).

BIRD'S EYE VIEW M.A.C. CAMPUS EAST LANSING, MICH.

Photo., only Copyright 1904 by the Rotograph Co.

Botanical and Bacteriological Laboratories, Agricultural College, Lansing, Mich.

BOT. LAB. & DAIRY BLDG. M. A. C. C.E.W.

Dairy and Entomology Buildings, Lansing, Mich. 15314

Campus View
Mich State College   Rex Photo

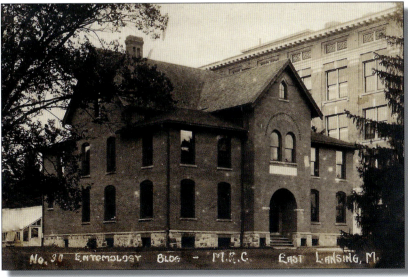

No. 30 Entomology Bldg - M.A.C.   East Lansing, M.

7928   Agricultural Building.
M. A. C. E. Lansing, Mich.   Pesha Ph

BIRD'S-EYE VIEW OF AGRICULTURA

EPARTMENT, M.A.C.

LYNDON
ANN ARBOR
MICH.

HORTICULTURE

Despite rapid growth of the college before and after World War I, the legislature provided funding for only two academic buildings between 1914 and 1925: Home Economics and Horticulture. Funds for Horticulture were appropriated in 1923. The building was built for the Horticulture Department, which previously had occupied an 1888 building built specifically for horticulture, using a design developed by Professor Liberty Hyde Bailey who led the program from 1885-1888. The 1888 building still stands nearby as part of the historic Laboratory Row, and is known as Eustace-Cole Hall.

Horticultural gardens once occupied the entire space east of Morrill Hall, extending all the way to Bogue Street. As the developed campus extended eastward in the early twentieth century, the garden areas shrank accordingly. Supported by greenhouses located behind the new building, they became demonstration gardens, showing ornamental plants and flowers to a wide array of visitors.

In 1986, both the Department of Horticulture and the gardens moved to the new Plant and Soil Sciences Building on South Campus. This building was renamed Old Horticulture. Following renovation it became the home of what are now known as the Department of French, Classics, and Italian and the Department of Spanish and Portuguese.

THE HORTICULTURAL BUILDING
EAST LANSING MICH.

EL-1   HORTICULTURE BUILDING, MICHIGAN STATE COLLEGE, EAST LANSING, MICHIGAN
© Rex Photo

Agricultural Laboratories. Lansing, Mich.

DAIRY

The Dairy Department began operation of a commercial dairy in the basement of the Agricultural Laboratory around 1900. The Agricultural Laboratory had become the Entomology Building by the time of this postcard in 1912. A year later, in 1901, the Dairy program moved into the new Dairy Building. The building included cold storage and cheese curing rooms, a "home dairy" room, a butter room and a cheese room, along with classrooms, offices, and laboratories. These buildings, known today as Chittenden and Cook Halls, both survive as a part of the historic Laboratory Row on West Circle Drive.

The 1901 facility was quickly outgrown, and a new Dairy Building was built in 1914 east of Agriculture Hall. This building had larger production facilities such as the Churn Room shown here. Students studied all aspects of dairy production and operations in these buildings and on the campus dairy farms.

Appropriately, the sender of one of these cards wrote to her mother, "Mrs. Hammond wants you to save 6 or 7 pounds of butter for next week." Another student writing home said "Prof wants us to go to a Butter Conference in Grand Rapids next week, but I can't go".

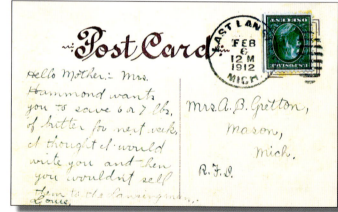

Hello Mother: Mrs. Hammond wants you to save 6 or 7 lbs. of butter for next week. I thought I would write you and then you wouldn't sell them to the Lansing man. Louie

THE CHURN ROOM
DAIRY BUILDING,
M.A.C.
EAST LANSING, MICH.
11-92

Dairy Building, M. A. C., Lansing, Mich.

FORESTRY BLDG. M.A.C.

For many years, the Dairy Store in this building was a popular place for ice cream cones. Students and visitors alike would line up on warm afternoons for a taste of campus-made ice creams. The Dairy Store is now found on Farm Lane south of Shaw Lane.

THE STOCK BARNS, M.A.C. EAST LANSING, MICH.

M.A.C.

C.E.W.

1955. DAIRY BARNS. M.A.C. EAST LANSING. MICH.

AGRICULTURE HALL

The first agricultural laboratory building on the campus was built in 1889 on what is now known as Laboratory Row. Rapid growth of the college caused the facility to quickly become inadequate. When Agriculture Hall opened in 1909, the agriculture laboratory was turned over to the Entomology Department. The building survives today and is known as Cook Hall.

The new Agriculture Hall, located on a site previously used for a cattle barn, was the largest building on the campus. It included a dirt-floored judging pavilion at the back which was used for classes and competitions. Also included was a farm engineering laboratory for instruction in use of the growing array of farm machinery. Because of its ceiling height and schedule availability, "The Spartan" statue was sculpted in the farm engineering laboratory in 1945 by Art Professor Leonard Jungwirth.

Ag Hall continues to house the offices of the College of Agriculture and related programs. It is one of the very few historic buildings on the campus to have been continuously occupied by the academic unit for which it was originally built.

Following the demolition of Morrill Hall in 2013, this building was renamed Morrill Hall of Agriculture honoring Senator Justin Morrill, author of the Land Grant Act of 1862, which created the system of "land grant" colleges and provided funding for them. The Michigan Agricultural College was the model for the Land Grant Act. Numerous land grant colleges around the country have a Morrill Hall.

New Agriculture Building. M.A.C. E. Lansing, Mich.

AGRICULTURAL BUILDING, MICHIGAN AGRICULTURAL COLLEGE, LANSING, MICH.

Agricultural Building M. A. C., Lansing, Mich.

P-12601

Agriculture Bldg. Mich. State College

FARM ENGINEERING LABORATORY M.A.C. EAST LANSING, MICH.

Stock Judging
M.A.C. 1913 Short Course

VETERINARY MEDICINE

V eterinary science was offered at MAC beginning in 1883, and the Veterinary Laboratory shown here was built in 1885. It was located in what is now the plaza area in front of the Hannah Administration Building.

A full-fledged veterinary degree program did not become a reality until 1910. Prior to that time, two private Veterinary Colleges, in Detroit and Grand Rapids, provided Michigan's veterinarians. In 1907, the Legislature authorized a veterinary science division at MAC, and by 1913 the Veterinary Clinic became a part of the landscape. Built at the corner of Farm Lane and East Circle Drive, the building received five additions between 1931 and 1968 and became the five-acre sprawling complex now known as Giltner Hall. The College of Veterinary Medicine left Giltner in 1965 for new quarters at Wilson Road and Bogue Street.

G 3819 Veterinary Laboratory, Agricultural College, Lansing, Mich.

A 3819 Veterinary Laboratory, Agricultural College, Lansing, Mich.

6/18/06 Lab.

No.20 Veterinary Building. M.A.C.

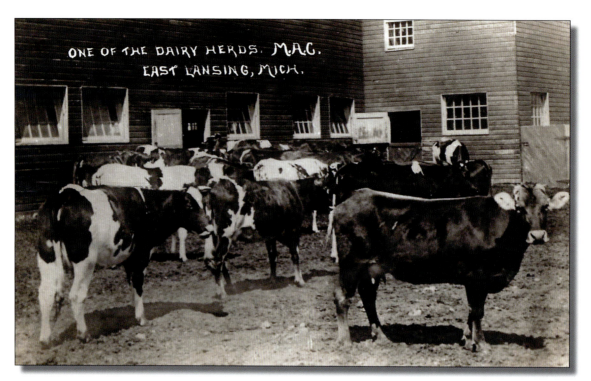

ONE OF THE DAIRY HERDS. M.A.C.
EAST LANSING, MICH.

Scene at M.A.C. East Lansing Mich.

ML206

FARM LANE M.A.C.

C.E.W.

RED CEDAR RIVER

CEDAR RIVER M.A.C. C.E.W.

What do you think of this? There are many places here just as fine.

CEDAR RIVER. M.A.C. C.E.W.

SCENE ON RED CEDAR RIVER M.A.C. East Lansing Mich.

Cedar River, M.A.C.

Cedar River, East Lansing. Mich.

Cedar River at Athletic Fields. E. Lansing, Mich.

VIEW OF THE DAM, M.A.C. No. 53

View on Cedar River, M. A. C., Lansing, Mich.

CANOEING ON THE RIVER

While an integral part of the campus from its beginning, the Red Cedar River's use for recreational purposes was apparently limited to fishing and the occasional dumping of freshmen until the early part of the twentieth century. Professor (and later President) Robert Shaw is reputed to have put the first canoe into the river in 1903. In short order, dozens of canoes owned by students appeared, and canoeing became a popular pastime. The young lady in this canoe wrote, "This was taken when I was in Lansing last week at the M. A. C."

The Canoe Shelter known to many students was a gift of the class of 1937. Prior to that time most canoes were privately owned.

Rec'd your card this noon and will write soon. This was taken when I was down Lansing last week at the M.A.C.

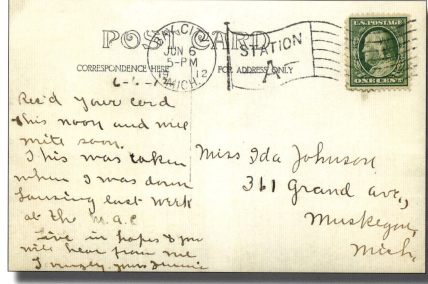

View on Cedar River, Agricultural College, Lansing, Mich.

Cedar R. above M.A.C. E. Lansing, Mi. 10350.

PREXY'S BLUFF. M.A.C. G.E.W.

BRIDGES

No. 8 Cedar River at M. A. C. Lansing, Mich.

With the main campus area north of the river and the farms to the south, bridges across the river were needed from the very beginning.

In his first annual report in 1858, President Williams noted that "Several of the students skilled in the use of tools, during last winter, unaided, erected a bridge across the Cedar River." The report does not identify the location of this early bridge, nor do early published campus maps identify it.

The first formal bridge appears in maps in the 1870s and crosses the Red Cedar at Farm Lane. In about 1888 a steel bridge replaced a wooden structure which had been designed by a member of the faculty. The view shown is from the south, prior to 1909. The smokestack is located near the present site of the Hannah Administration Building. Note that Ag Hall had not yet been built and that the surrounding area is covered with barns and other farm buildings. The bridge is in use by its most frequent users—farm animals—whose barns were north

View from Farm Lane, M. A. C. Lansing, Mich.

Engineering Bldg. M.A.C. from Cedar River. E. Lansing, Mich.

Foot Bridge and Cedar River M.A.C., Lansing, Mich.

of the river and pastures to the south. This bridge stood until 1928, when it was replaced by the present structure.

In 1901, the Pere Marquette Railroad built a railroad extension from Trowbridge to the campus boiler house north of the river. The bridge crossed near the present Library and Olds Hall, and was used to carry coal to the boiler house, which consumed 3-4,000 tons of coal each year. The bridge also permitted excursion trains to visit the campus and was used extensively for this purpose in the early 1900s. The view here notes that it was much more than just a railroad bridge, as it was the only pedestrian crossing between the Farm Lane Bridge and the one at the Spartan Statue until the 1940s. It was demolished in 1968.

A wooden pedestrian and vehicular bridge accessing the college athletic fields (the Kalamazoo Street Bridge) was built in 1903. This bridge was dynamited in 1926 to clear an ice backup which was creating a major flood upstream on the campus.

Today there are 10 bridges over the Red Cedar River between Hagadorn Road to the east and Kalamazoo Street to the west.

Bridge over Red Cedar River. M.A.C. East Lansing, Mich.

Cedar River Bridge M.A.C. East Lansing, Mich. Photo

Farm Lane, M.A.C.

Barns, M.A.C. C.E.W.

How are you brother and all your studies? I can't tell when I will be home.

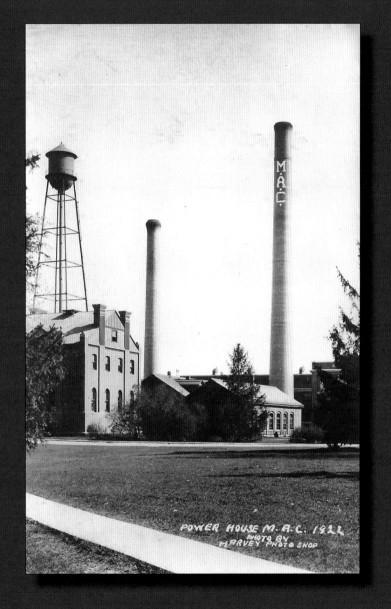

POWER HOUSE M. A. C. 1922
PHOTO BY
HARVEY PHOTO SHOP

CAMPUS SUPPORT

SMOKESTACKS

For many years, visitors to the campus have been fascinated by the three smokestacks describing the history of the growth of the college. The first stack, shown in this view, was built in 1904 and had the familiar MAC set into the chimney with tan colored brick. The power house was located behind the veterinary clinic, north of the river.

The second stack was built in 1948 at the Shaw Lane plant. At this time, the new plant was the only major permanent building south of the Red Cedar other than athletic buildings. Appropriately for its time, the stack carried the MSC letters on both the north and south sides of the stack.

The third stack was built at the new T. B. Simon Power Plant on Service Road in 1965. Like the Shaw Lane stack, it has the MSU letters in white brick on both the north and south sides.

The three stacks stood together for a fairly brief period as highly visible monuments to the growth of the college and its evolution to the great university of today. About a year after completion of the MSU stack in 1965, the old MAC stack was removed, along with the power plant, to make room for the new Hannah Administration Building. The steam tunnels which radiated out from this plant to the major campus buildings were not removed, however, and still converge at the site of the old plant. The MSC stack at the Shaw Lane Plant was removed in recent years, leaving only the MSU stack and its newer twin at the Simon Plant.

STEAM TUNNELS

Early campus buildings were lit with oil lamps and heated with wood stoves. It is not surprising that many of the early buildings were destroyed by fire. With the spread of electric power and central steam heating systems, newer, safer means of heating and lighting were available.

Out of necessity, the remote MAC campus created its own power generation and heating system. In 1904, a central heating, lighting and power system was built. A central plant was constructed in front of the current location of the Hannah Administration Building, with steam tunnels radiating out to all of the major buildings. The tunnels, many of which are still in use, are about six feet high and carried steam, water, power and telephone lines. The tall smokestack, with the letters MAC set in the brick of the smokestack, was a campus landmark for many years.

The new plant replaced most of the coal and wood-burning heating systems around the campus, and in his 1915 history of MAC, Professor W. J. Beal noted of the new plant that "the absence of smoke from the chimney is very much appreciated by the dwellers on the campus."

The plant was the main source of heat and power for the campus until it was replaced in 1948 by the Shaw Lane Plant. The plant and smokestack were razed in the 1960s to make way for the Hannah Administration Building. The tunnels still converge at the former site of the plant, and an entrance door to their point of convergence can be found in front of one of the gardens in the Administration Building Plaza.

Half-Way Rock between Capitol
and M. A. C., Lansing, Mich

OFF CAMPUS HOUSING

At its opening in 1857, the college's remote location mandated that virtually everyone live in facilities located on the campus. Faculty homes were built on Faculty Row, dormitories were constructed for students, and apartments and rooming houses for faculty assistants, extension agents, and their families.

Growth in enrollment combined with loss of student housing caused by the burning of two dormitories created a demand for student housing which could not be met on campus. The addition of a women's program in 1896 resulted in conversion of Abbot Hall from men's housing to women. Faced with growing enrollment and an inability to expand the on-campus supply of housing, male students were encouraged to live off-campus. In fact, in 1896 a faculty committee recommended elimination of all dormitories. The recommendation was not accepted.

THE COLUMBIAN CLUB M.A.C. EAST LANSING MICH. 11-56

At the same time, faculty opposed recognizing the national fraternities, voting to terminate Delta Tau Delta in 1896. Phi Delta Theta, the only other fraternity, voted to reorganize as a local society in 1898. It was not until 1921 that the ban was lifted.

Most undergraduate men lived off campus in the early years of the twentieth century. Some lived in private homes, others in hotels and rooming houses, and a growing number in society houses which filled the gap caused by the ban on national fraternities and sororities. Many took their meals at the handful of off campus restaurants in the East Lansing community.

The new Columbian Literary Society house on Bogue Street near Grand River opened in 1914. The house accommodated thirty students on the second and third floors and had a bathroom for each floor. Two of the bathrooms were equipped with a shower.

Some of the literary society houses later became fraternity and sorority houses after 1921.

SPLIT ROCK

In the early days, MAC was a long 3½ mile walk from Lansing on a dirt road. On Saturday afternoons, it was not uncommon for students to make the trip from campus to Lansing and back to visit the only "big city" in the area. On the way, a common resting point was a large boulder which had been split by a cherry tree. Known as Split Rock or Halfway Rock, it was located at the intersection of Kipling Boulevard and Michigan Avenue, where the trolley line ended.

The site became a sentimental landmark for students and a common reference point for travel. In the 1920s, Michigan Avenue became a boulevard and the site was paved over. The rock became truly split, with one part moved to the campus grounds and the remaining part dispersed in pieces throughout the community.

SPLIT ROCK, LANSING, MICH.

SEMI-CENTENNIAL CELEBRATION

SEMI-CENTENNIAL

The Semi-Centennial celebration took place in June of 1907, fifty years after the dedication of College Hall and the start of the first classes. Enrollment had grown to 693 students, plus an additional 140 in a "sub-freshman" curriculum designed for those students who had not completed high school. A high school diploma did not become a requirement for admission to the college until 1915.

Twenty thousand people came to the campus to hear President Theodore Roosevelt deliver a speech titled "The Man Who Works with His Hands." R. E. Olds won a coin toss in President Snyder's office and drove the President to the campus from Lansing in a new REO automobile manufactured in Lansing. Roosevelt returned to the train station in Lansing in an Oldsmobile driven by the man who lost the toss.

The President's visit was not without problems. During a parade from the Capitol to the campus, there was a lengthy delay. Four or five members of the college band went on strike, refusing to march without being paid. The band marched without them.

President Roosevelt addressing students and Alumni at M. A. C., Graduating Exercises and 50th Anniversary Celebration, May 31st, 1907.

During the President's speech, an explosion sent a ripple of fear through the crowd, and a security force was dispatched to locate the cause. The source of the explosion was never found. However, after the event a small group of students was charged with detonating a powder keg and dismissed from school.

One of the dismissed students, Forest Akers of Williamston, got a job as salesman for Olds and went on to a highly successful career in the rapidly growing auto industry. Despite the fact that he denied being the culprit and never returned to MAC to complete his degree, his interest in the college continued throughout his lifetime. He was elected to the State Board of Agriculture (now the MSU Board of Trustees) in 1939 and served until 1957. He was a major donor during his lifetime, providing funding for the University's two golf courses, and he left his entire estate to a trust dedicated to the welfare of the students at MSU.

THE MAN WHO WORKS WITH HIS HANDS

Excerpts from the Address of President Roosevelt at the Semi-Centennial Celebration of the Founding of Agricultural Colleges in the United States at Lansing, Mich., May 31, 1907.

THE MAN WHO WORKS WITH HIS HANDS.

The fiftieth anniversary of the founding of this college is an event of national significance, for Michigan was the first State in the Union to found this, the first agricultural college in America. The Nation is to be congratulated on the fact that the Congress at Washington has repeatedly enacted laws designed to aid the several States in establishing and maintaining agricultural and mechanical colleges. I greet all such colleges, through their representatives who have gathered here today, and bid them Godspeed in their work. I no less heartily invoke success for the mechanical and agricultural schools...

THE FARMER IN RELATION TO THE WELFARE OF THE WHOLE COUNTRY.

There is but one person whose welfare is as vital to the welfare of the whole country as is that of the wage-worker who does manual labor; and that is the tiller of the soil—the farmer. If there is one lesson taught by history it is that the permanent greatness of any State must ultimately depend more upon the character of its country population than upon anything else. No growth of cities, no growth of wealth, can make up for a loss in either the number or the character of the farming population. In the United States more than in almost any other country we should realize this and should prize our country population. When this Nation began its independent existence it as was a Nation of farmers. The towns were small and were for the most part mere seacoast trading and fishing ports. The chief industry of the country was agriculture, and the ordinary citizen was in some way connected with it. In every great crisis of the past a peculiar dependence has had to be placed upon the farming population; and this dependence has hitherto been justified. But it cannot be justified in the future if agriculture is permitted to sink in the scale as compared with other employments. We cannot afford to lose that preeminently typical American, the farmer who owns his own farm.

KIND OF EDUCATION NEEDED.

Agricultural colleges and farmers' institutes have done much in instruction and inspiration; they have stood for the nobility of labor and the necessity of keeping the muscles and the brain in training for industry. They have developed technical departments of high practical value. They seek to provide for the people on the farms an equipment so broad and thorough as to fit them for the highest requirements of our citizenship; so that they can establish and maintain country homes of the best type, and create and sustain a country civilization more than equal to that of the city. The men they train must be able to meet the strongest business competition, at home or abroad, and they can do this only if they are trained not alone in the various lines of husbandry but in successful economic management. These colleges, like the State experiment stations, should carefully study and make known the needs of each section, and should try to provide remedies for what is wrong.

The education to be obtained in these colleges should create as intimate relationship as is possible between the theory of learning and the facts of actual life. Educational establishments should produce highly trained scholars, of course; but in a country like ours, where the educational establishments are so numerous, it is folly to think that their main purpose is to produce these highly trained scholars. Without in the least disparaging scholarship and learning – on the contrary, while giving hearty and ungrudging admiration and support to the comparatively few whose primary work should be creative scholarship – it must be remembered that the ordinary graduate of our colleges should be and must be, primarily, a man and not a scholar. Education should not confine itself to books. It must train executive power, and try to create that right public opinion which is the most potent factor in the proper solution of all political and social questions. Book-learning is very important, but it is by no means everything; and we shall never get the right idea of education until we definitely understand that a man may be well trained in book-learning and yet, in the proper sense of the word, and for all practical purposes, be utterly uneducated; while a man of comparatively little book-learning may, nevertheless, in essentials have a good education.

ABOUT THE AUTHOR

Stephen Terry is a 1960 graduate of Michigan State University. Upon graduation he spent six years with a national CPA firm before returning to the campus where he stayed until his retirement in 1998. For most of that time, he was the University's Senior Financial Officer.

He began collecting MSU memorabilia at age seventeen, when he was admitted to the University. His grandmother gave him an 1877 catalog of the Agricultural College where his great-grandfather graduated. He began collecting MSU postcards in the 1980s and currently has a collection of about 1,000 cards from throughout the university's history, beginning in the early 1900s when the picture post card era began.

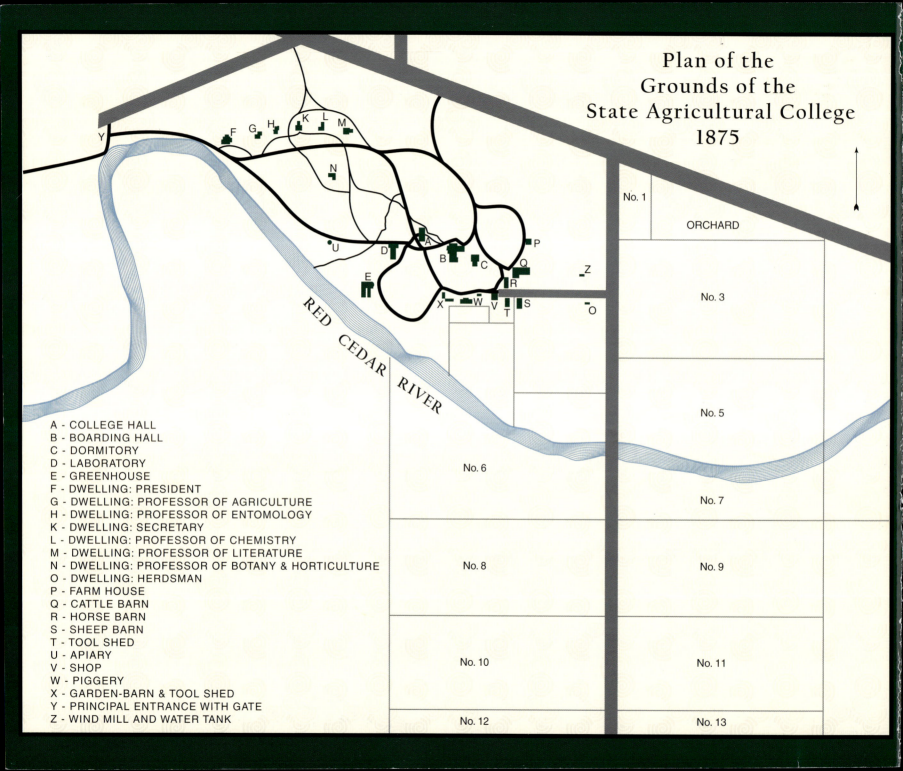

Plan of the Grounds of the State Agricultural College 1875

RED CEDAR RIVER

ORCHARD

No. 1
No. 3
No. 5
No. 6
No. 7
No. 8
No. 9
No. 10
No. 11
No. 12
No. 13

A - COLLEGE HALL
B - BOARDING HALL
C - DORMITORY
D - LABORATORY
E - GREENHOUSE
F - DWELLING: PRESIDENT
G - DWELLING: PROFESSOR OF AGRICULTURE
H - DWELLING: PROFESSOR OF ENTOMOLOGY
K - DWELLING: SECRETARY
L - DWELLING: PROFESSOR OF CHEMISTRY
M - DWELLING: PROFESSOR OF LITERATURE
N - DWELLING: PROFESSOR OF BOTANY & HORTICULTURE
O - DWELLING: HERDSMAN
P - FARM HOUSE
Q - CATTLE BARN
R - HORSE BARN
S - SHEEP BARN
T - TOOL SHED
U - APIARY
V - SHOP
W - PIGGERY
X - GARDEN-BARN & TOOL SHED
Y - PRINCIPAL ENTRANCE WITH GATE
Z - WIND MILL AND WATER TANK